DEVELOPING
SPIRITUAL
ACCURACY

DEVELOPING SPIRITUAL ACCURACY

How to Sharpen Your Discernment Level to Flow With God's Leading

Dr. John A. Tetsola

Developing Spiritual Accuracy
How to Sharpen Your Discernment Level To Flow With God's Leading

ISBN 0-9634306-0-2

Note: In some Scripture quotations, italics have been added by the author for emphasis only.

Table of Contents

CHAPTER ONE

UNDERSTANDING SPIRITUAL ACCURACY

Developing spiritual accuracy is paramount for the church today. The Body of Christ must learn accuracy in the spirit in order to effectively hear and sense what God is saying in these last days. For many years, the church has demonstrated inaccuracy in almost everything she has done. There have been believers, from generation to generation, who have inaccurately discerned the movement of the Spirit of God. Many Christians have been led astray because of this, and the church is still experiencing this same predicament today. Part of this problem is attributed to men and women who have not been thoroughly trained in how to hear, sense, and pinpoint what God is saying.

For every movement that has come and gone, there have always been men and women — a remnant — who have possessed a high degree of sensitivity and who have accurately forecasted the coming of these movements or "waves" before they even arrived. These very individuals understood and demonstrated spiritual accuracy, because they were connected to the spiritual realm and they could tell what God was saying. God is calling in this hour for a higher quality and caliber of men and women, through whom He can speak and who He can depend on. The Body of Christ is in great need of accurate men and women in leadership positions, people who will not assume, but who will listen and receive what God is saying. The church needs accurate apostles, prophets, teachers, evangelists and pastors, who can pinpoint the very mind of God.

The church is tired of inaccurate men and women tending God's pulpits. There is a cry and a great search for individuals who are accurate in the ways of God. It is a great tragedy to be led by an inaccurate leader. An inaccurate ministry will produce inaccurate babies. God is not looking for "guessing Christians" in these last days. He is looking for spiritual forecasters — men and women who can forecast and tell what is about to happen. God is looking for believers who are accurate in their spiritual meteorology, believers who can rightly predict and sense the spiritual storm before its arrival. These are the bunch that God is calling for today.

Spiritual accuracy involves extreme precision and exactness, which is the condition of being accurate. It involves being free from error, defect and mistake. It has to do with being strictly correct and adhering to exactness. This is powerful! This is what the Spirit of God is calling for today in the church. God is in need of a people that will be free from error, defect and mistake, but not perfect, in receiving and operating in His gifts. God wants Christians that will be extremely precise and exact in adhering to His commandments.

The Race of Certainty

> Know ye not that they which run in a race run all, but one receiveth the prize? So run, that ye may obtain.

And every man that striveth for the mastery is temperate in all things. Now they do it to obtain a corruptible crown; but we an incorruptible.

I therefore so run, not as uncertainly; so fight I, not as one that beateth the air:

But I keep under my body, and bring it into subjection: lest that by any means, when I have preached to others, I myself should be a castaway.

1 Corinthians 9:24-27

Whether we realize it or not, the Christian experience is a race. It is a race that needs to be run with exactness and free of error and defect in order to be successful. In order to receive the prize of the race, the church must run the Christian race with accuracy. Mastery is demanded in order to be successful.

Paul said, when he runs, he runs not with uncertainty. A believer that is uncertain is one that is unsure of what he or she is doing and where he or she is going. He or she is one that is definitely unsettled, unfixed and undetermined. Such individuals are not accurate. The individual does not know if he or she is right or wrong. This is a very sad condition to be in. Paul also said that when he fights, he does not fight as one who beats the air. We have a lot of air-beating Christians. They are not certain, fixed, or sure of what they are doing.

Can you imagine a boxer in the ring with an opponent punching him and he is just beating the air? Instead of punching and beating his opponent, he punches the air. This immediately tells you that the boxer has problems with his punch. He needs to go back to the drawing board. He needs to go back to the gymnasium to accurately sharpen his punching skills.

A lot of believers are in the same boat today. They are never accurate in receiving messages from God. Their ministering, preaching and teaching are always off the target because they have not developed the spirit of accuracy. They are in the spiritual ring punching, but always beating the air. They are never accurate in their punches. The enemy is never the target. Surprisingly, we have leaders and ministers leading great churches and congregations, yet they fall into this category. It is not surprising that many Christians have been led astray because of these inaccurate leaders and ministers.

Running With Purpose in Every Step

God needs believers who are certain; believers that are absolutely sure, convinced, settled, fixed and determined in what they are doing and saying. God needs fighters that can accurately punch. Not fighters that hit below the belt, but fighters who will listen and strictly adhere to the guidance and instruction of their "managers."

Let's look at what the Living Bible says about this:

> **So I run straight to the goal with purpose in every step. I fight to win. I'm not just shadowboxing or playing around.**
>
> **1 Corinthians 9:26 TLB**

Look carefully at what Paul said here. He said, "I run straight to the goal with purpose in every step." A believer that possesses the spirit of accuracy is always aware of his purpose. That is one of the reasons they are dangerous to the enemy. They are not confused or mixed up. They are very directional in their walk. Did you notice the word "straight?" Paul was concerned about accuracy. He was straight in his race. He knew where he was going. He knew how to locate the goal and that the goal would lead him to the purpose of God. He learned, developed, and possessed the spirit of accuracy.

Shadow Boxers

I fight to win. I'm not just shadowboxing or playing around.

1 Corinthians 9:26b TLB

Look at what Paul had to say. I fight to win. I am not just shadowboxing or playing around. Isn't this interesting? A man that fights to win is a man who is accurate in his purpose. We have a lot of shadowboxing ministers and believers in the Body of Christ. All they do is box their own shadow. All they see are shadows and never reality. The ways of God are never real to them.

The Spirit of Micaiah

Then the king of Israel gathered the prophets together, about four hundred men, and said unto them, Shall I go against Ramothgilead to battle, or shall I forbear? And they said, Go up; for the Lord shall deliver *it* into the hand of the king.

And Micaiah said, *As* the LORD liveth, what the LORD saith unto me, that will I speak.

And he said, Hear thou therefore the word of the LORD: I saw the LORD sitting on his throne, and all the host of heaven standing by him on his right hand and on his left.

And the LORD said, Who shall persuade Ahab, that he may go up and fall at Ramothgilead? And one said on this manner, and another said on that manner.

And there came forth a spirit, and stood before the LORD, and said, I will persuade him.

And the LORD said unto him, Wherewith? And he said, I will go forth, and I will be a lying spirit in the mouth of all his prophets. And he said, Thou shalt persuade *him*, and prevail also: go forth, and do so.

Now therefore, behold, the LORD hath put a lying spirit in the mouth of all these thy prophets, and the LORD hath spoken evil concerning thee.

But Zedekiah the son of Chenaanah went near, and smote Micaiah on the cheek, and said, Which way went the Spirit of the LORD from me to speak unto thee?

And Micaiah said, Behold, thou shalt see in that day, when thou shalt go into an inner chamber to hide thyself.

And Micaiah said, If thou return at all in peace, the LORD hath not spoken by me. And he said, Hearken, O people, every one of you.

1 Kings 22:6, 14, 19-25, 28

The prophet Micaiah was an example of a prophet that exhibited the spirit of accuracy in his ministry and his walk with God. Micaiah, as a prophet, was called upon to predict and determine what the outcome of the war of Ramoth in Gilead between Israel and Syria would be. The Bible lets us know about the prophecy that was made by the prophets of Baal. The Word of the Lord from these prophets of Baal was inaccurate. The true spirit of accuracy comes from the presence of God.

They could not locate on God's spiritual map what the outcome of the battle would be, despite several efforts. We have individuals today with the same spirit of Baal. All they do is prophesy inaccurate words. Prophesying is right, but giving inaccurate words is wrong. Ministries, homes, and families have been destroyed by inaccurate words of direction from men and women who do not possess the spirit of accuracy.

Speaking the Heart of God

Look at what the prophet Micaiah said: "As the Lord liveth, what the Lord saith unto me, that will I speak." The church needs more people with the spirit of Micaiah, men who are only concerned about what God has to say and not about themselves. Micaiah made up his mind, and said that he would only say what the Lord had spoken to him. He refused to say anything less or anything more.

Despite the efforts of the prophet Zedekiah and the other prophets of Baal to persuade him to change his mind, Micaiah made sure that the true Word of the Lord was released. I love what he said in verse 19. He said, "hear thou therefore the word of the Lord: I saw the Lord sitting on His throne...." This is a statement of accuracy. Micaiah said *I saw the Lord sitting on His throne.* He was not inaccurate. He knew what he saw. He was able to pinpoint what he saw. He was able to describe his experience. It was crystal clear to him. This is the kind of accuracy that God is calling for today — words, messages, and teachings that are exact and free from error and mistake. God is calling for men and women who will be accurate in releasing the Word of the Lord.

Spiritual Ladders and Stairways

> **And he lighted upon a certain place, and tarried there all night, because the sun was set; and he took of the stones of that place, and put *them for* his pillows, and lay down in that place to sleep.**
>
> **And he dreamed, and behold a ladder set up on the earth, and the top of it reached to heaven: and behold the angels of God ascending and descending on it.**
>
> **And, behold, the LORD stood above it, and said, I *am* the LORD God of Abraham thy father, and the God of Isaac: the land whereon thou liest, to thee will I give it, and to thy seed;**
>
> **Genesis 28:11-13**

There is no better illustration of spiritual accuracy than the experience of Jacob. The Bible lets us know that in obeying his father concerning who to marry, Jacob came to the city called Luz. While at Luz, Jacob had a dream in which he saw a ladder set up on the earth. The Hebrew word for ladder is *sullam* which means to pile up like terraces or a stairway. In other words, Jacob saw a stairway and the top of it reached heaven, while the angels of God were ascending and descending upon it. And the Lord stood above the stairway. This is a very beautiful picture of spiritual accuracy. This is exactly what God is calling for and demanding in this reformation. He wants men and women who will climb the stairway or ladder of heaven to receive His heart for His people. Accuracy comes from connecting and linking with heaven's ladder or stairway. The heart of God is the source of every accuracy.

We have a lot of Christians who want to possess and operate in the spirit of accuracy, yet they are too lazy to press in and climb the ladder or stairway connecting heaven to earth. Spiritual accuracy is of the spirit realm. It is not of the physical realm. Inaccuracy is of the physical realm and not of the spirit realm. God wants to speak profoundly to His people in these last days, but He needs men and women who will not be lazy to climb heaven's stairway or ladder to receive His accurate Word for His people. He needs men who are divinely connected and linked to heaven. As the church begins to climb God's stairway or ladder, God, on the other side, will begin to send prophetic words to His people. This generation will witness and experience the angelic ascension and descension with the Word of the Lord for God's people like never before.

Stages of Accuracy

Paul made three outstanding statements during his entire Christian life that helped to define, locate and identify the various levels and stages of spiritual accuracy during his life and ministry. We will examine each of these statements as we go further.

And he trembling and astonished said, Lord, what wilt thou have me to do? And the Lord

said unto him, Arise, and go into the city, and it shall be told thee what thou must do.

Acts 9:6

For the which cause I also suffer these things: nevertheless I am not ashamed: for I know whom I have believed, and am persuaded that he is able to keep that which I have committed unto him against that day.

2 Timothy 1:12

I have fought a good fight, I have finished *my* course, I have kept the faith:

2 Timothy 4:7

The above Scriptures will help to explain some of the stages and levels of spiritual accuracy. Before spiritual accuracy is fully achieved, the believer or individual must go through three stages: the ignorance stage, the learning stage, and the acceptance or fulfillment stage. Spiritual accuracy is not achieved overnight. There are metamorphic processes that are undergone and required before spiritual accuracy is fully operational.

The Ignorance Stage

And he trembling and astonished said, Lord, what wilt thou have me to do? And the Lord *said* unto him, Arise, and go into the city, and it shall be told thee what thou must do.

Acts 9:6

This is the stage where the individual has neither knowledge nor understanding of how to operate properly and accurately. Every believer must experience this level or stage before realizing proper operation of the spirit of accuracy. This is the level or stage of initiation and introduction of the spirit of accuracy. A great deal of inaccuracy is permitted in this level because it is the stage of ignorance. We have a lot of Christians and leaders who cannot afford to accept their ignorance concerning certain areas of the ways of God. They portray great impressions of knowledge and understanding in almost every area of the ways of God, and yet their ignorance is obvious. There is nothing wrong in being at this stage, as long as you don't remain here.

Paul's question, *"Lord what wilt thou have me to do?"* was a statement of uncertainty. It revealed his ignorance concerning the purpose of God for his life. Remember that the spirit of accuracy involves extreme exactness and surety, which is the condition of being free from error and defect. Paul, in this case, was unsure of what God wanted him to do. He was still ignorant concerning how to find the purpose of God for his destiny. He was inaccurate in locating the will of God for his life.

The Learning Stage

For the which cause I also suffer these things: nevertheless I am not ashamed: for I know whom I have believed, and am persuaded that he is able to keep that which I have committed unto him against that day.

2 Timothy 1:12

This Scripture deals with the second level which I call the learning stage. This is the awareness stage of the spirit of accuracy without a full mastery of it. It is also a stage of mistakes and errors. Inaccuracy is allowed and permitted in this level because it involves a great deal of learning. Many Christians want to become accurate in everything they do, yet they do not want to learn what it takes to be accurate in the spirit. This group of believers wants to operate in the spirit of accuracy, yet they are not ready to make mistakes. Mastery is not achieved overnight. It comes with practice and with time. It comes with mistakes and blunders. But the main issue is, in spite of the mistakes and errors, the individual must not give up. He must continue to strive for mastery. The Scripture says that a righteous man falls seven times and he still gets up.

Paul's statement, "For I know whom I have believed and I am persuaded that He is able to keep that which I have committed unto Him against that day," portrayed an element of surety and accuracy, but not in full propensity. Paul's statement in this Scripture drew a clear picture of what his spiritual state was. A great disparity can be seen from the pictures drawn between his statement made while he was in the ignorance stage and the learning stage.

The Fulfillment Stage

I have fought a good fight, I have finished *my* course, I have kept the faith:

2 Timothy 4:7

The fulfillment and acceptance stage of spiritual accuracy actually involves the achievement of mastery. Here the degree, frequency, and number of errors and mistakes are extremely low. Mistakes are made once in a while, but in a very small magnitude. They are not made constantly or consistently.

Paul's statement, "I have fought a good fight, I have finished my course" shows his level or stage of growth at this time in his Christian walk. For him to complete his "course" would mean that somewhere along the line he was able to locate the proper direction, expected procedure, proper conduct, and policy that would enable him to accurately pursue the purpose of God for his life without any mistakes and errors.

These three stages or levels of spiritual accuracy remind me of two sporting events in which you may witness the same various stages (ignorance, learning, and acceptance or fulfillment).

Take, for example, a youngster who signs up for little league (sandlot league) baseball and all he knows about the sport is that his father purchased a bat and glove for him to use. As he makes his first attempts at batting, he swings amiss, never making contact with the ball. As time goes on, he becomes older and a little more mature about the game, and he finally makes initial "contact" with the ball.

His missing the ball is far more frequent than making contact, but hitting the "target" is being achieved. Through further development, the percentage of "targets" being hit exceeds the number of misses. It is at this acceptance stage that persistence and perfection must be strived for. Finally, this baseball player is hitting everything that comes his way. The percentage of hit "targets" has reached a hundred, while misses are unheard of.

Quite similarly, let's observe the sport of archery. At first, archers quite often find themselves shooting an arrow at a target and never hitting it. After much time and practice has been spent, the soon-to-be archers begin hitting the target periodically more often than the times that they miss. The archers become more "accurate" in their attempts. Even though there are some misses, they are few and far between.

Finally, at last the archers have stepped up to a level where hitting the target is the norm. The perfection now lies in how many times the bull's-eye is hit. This individual has stepped up to become a true "marksman!"

The church needs to be spiritually quick and brisk, clear and distinct; to be vigilant, attentive, and to have a keen perception of the movement, ways, and direction of the Spirit of God today. God wants His people to comprehend and interpret what He is saying and doing. He wants His people to develop a keen perception in this reformation.

The Place Called Zuph

> **And when they were come to the land of Zuph, Saul said to his servant that *was* with him, Come, and let us return; lest my father leave *caring* for the asses, and take thought for us.**
>
> **And he said unto him, Behold now, *there is* in this city a man of God, and *he is* an honourable man; all that he saith cometh surely to pass: now let us go thither; peradventure he can shew us our way that we should go.**
>
> **1 Samuel 9:5-6**

There was something about this city. This was the place of new direction for Saul and his servant. It was the take-off point of purpose finding. Even though Saul did not know what was going on in the spirit realm or what was about to happen to him, God had ordained that a divine connection between Saul and Samuel would flow out of this city. The city of Zuph brought an end to Saul's search for the beasts of burden. When an individual comes to that place of new direction, a purpose is birthed. Most Christians today need some new fresh direction. Most believers have been on a search too long. It is difficult for them to see and understand clearly. If you are pursuing the wrong thing, it is very difficult to see and understand clearly. All that is needed is a fresh new anointing which will point you in the direction of God.

Even though Saul was in Zuph, he still did not understand the importance of that city. He did not know the kind of anointing that was in that city. He forgot that the prophet Samuel lived in that very city. It was not that Samuel was unpopular. He was popular. He was the priest that replaced the house of Eli. He was, more or less, the ruler of Israel at this time. So, it was surprising that Saul did not understand that he was in the right city.

The Power of Recognition

> And he said unto him, Behold now, *there is* in this city a man of God, and *he is* an honourable man; all that he saith cometh surely to pass: now let us go thither; peradventure he can shew us our way that we should go.

1 Samuel 9:6

Thank God for good servants and friends like Saul's servant. Sometimes you need a good friend, a good leader, and minister to help put you on the right course and direction. The blind cannot effectively lead the blind. It is not possible.

The Body of Christ needs people who are not blind to the ways of God, people who can see, hear, understand and be able to pinpoint what God is saying and doing in the land today. Saul's servant was able to spiritually pinpoint the anointing in the city of Zuph. He was able to locate that there was man of God in the city. The servant was able to know that the man of God was an honorable man and he was able to pinpoint that all that the man of God said surely came to pass. Every believer needs friends, leaders, and ministers like that—friends, leaders, and ministers who will be spiritually quick and brisk, clear and distinct. We need men and women who are very attentive to the direction of the Spirit of God and who constantly and consistently have a spiritually keen perception concerning the movement, acts, and ways of God.

> **Then said Saul to his servant, But, behold, *if* we go, what shall we bring the man? for the bread is spent in our vessels, and *there is* not a present to bring to the man of God: what have we?**
>
> **1 Samuel 9:7**

Saul, with all of the persuasion from his servant, was still looking for excuses not to see the prophet Samuel. We have people today who will make and give every excuse in the book not to participate or partake in this reformation of the Spirit of God.

> **And the servant answered Saul again, and said, Behold, I have here at hand the fourth part of a shekel of silver: *that* will I give to the man of God, to tell us our way.**
>
> **1 Samuel 9:8**

The servant himself was persistent. Despite Saul's excuse to withdraw, the servant was still able to put him on the right course by saying, "Behold I have here at hand the fourth part of a shekel of silver."

Spirit of the Armor Bearer

Looking at Saul and his servant, I immediately see the spirit of an armor bearer here in operation in the life of Saul's servant. He knew how to serve his master. He was able to lead his master into the place of insight. There is great fear today among many pastors and leaders that their associates, assistants, or servants are out to steal their flock. As a result of this, there is no trust between the pastors or leaders and their associates. I believe that God has someone prepared for every pastor and leader.

The Role of the Armor Bearer

Saul's servant, because of his commitment to his master, was able to provide strength for his master. He had a sense of respect for his master and acceptance for and tolerance of his master's personality and his ways of doing things. He made the advancement of his master his main priority. He was able to minister strength and courage to his master. He was able to awaken and arouse his master's insight. He was able to rescue his master from difficulty and hardship. He was able to prepare and care for his master's needs. He anticipated his master's needs, and was able to properly furnish and supply what was needed. He was able to bring acceleration in growth and promotion to his master. He was able to complete and complement his leader.

An Encounter With the Sprit of Reformation

> And the servant answered Saul again, and said,
> Behold, I have here at hand the fourth part of a
> shekel of silver: *that* will I give to the man of
> God, to tell us our way.
>
> Now the LORD had told Samuel in his ear a
> day before Saul came, saying,
>
> To morrow about this time I will send thee a
> man out of the land of Benjamin, and thou shalt
> anoint him *to be* captain over my people Israel,
> that he may save my people out of the hand of
> the Philistines: for I have looked upon my
> people, because their cry is come unto me.
>
> And Samuel answered Saul, and said, I *am* the
> seer: go up before me unto the high place; for
> ye shall eat with me to day, and to morrow I
> will let thee go, and will tell thee all that *is* in
> thine heart.
>
> And as for thine asses that were lost three days
> ago, set not thy mind on them; for they are
> found. And on whom *is* all the desire of Israel?
> *Is it* not on thee, and on all thy father's house?
>
> **1 Samuel 9:10, 15-16, 19-20**

Saul finally agreed to see the man of God (the prophet Samuel). Saul's encounter with the prophet Samuel changed his entire life and ministry. Saul was never the same again. He was changed from a burden searcher to a purposeful leader. An encounter with the Spirit of God will change your life. Most Christians remain unchanged because they have not had an encounter with the anointing. There has never been anyone who has had an encounter with the anointing of God and has remained the same. The strength of the Spirit of

God will change your life, your ministry, your church, and your old starchy and rigid forms of worship—when it is properly embraced. The anointing of God, when embraced, will destroy every yoke of tradition; it will destroy every man-made protocol, and pull down every man-imputed burden.

> **And as for thine asses that were lost three days ago, set not thy mind on them; for they are found. And on whom *is* all the desire of Israel? *Is it* not on thee, and on all thy father's house?**

1 Samuel 9:20

Without Saul telling the prophet Samuel of his mission and intentions, Samuel was able to spiritually pinpoint, with a one hundred percent degree of accuracy, the lost asses. This is what the church will see and experience in this movement of the Spirit of God. A high degree of accurate pinpointing will be in full operation. Without any problem men and women will be able to pinpoint the movement and things of God on God's spiritual map. The time of guessing is over. The season of spiritual accuracy is here to stay! God is doing something new in the land today. God is in need of men and women who will be willing to pay the price to walk in spiritual accuracy in Him.

God is training "spiritual meteorologists," while developing their skills of "spiritual forecasting." God's spiritual map is open and accessible to the church today. All God needs is men and women who will be able to interpret, comprehend, and spiritually pinpoint the place, position, direction, and flow of His Spirit to His people.

The Blessings of a New Anointing

Then Samuel took a vial of oil, and poured *it* upon his head, and kissed him, and said, *Is it* not because the LORD hath anointed thee *to be* captain over his inheritance?

When thou art departed from me to day, then thou shalt find two men by Rachel's sepulchre in the border of Benjamin at Zelzah; and they will say unto thee, The asses which thou wentest to seek are found: and, lo, thy father hath left the care of the asses, and sorroweth for you, saying, What shall I do for my son?

Then shalt thou go on forward from thence, and thou shalt come to the plain of Tabor, and there shall meet thee three men going up to God to Bethel, one carrying three kids, and another carrying three loaves of bread, and another carrying a bottle of wine:

And they will salute thee, and give thee two *loaves* of bread; which thou shalt receive of their hands.

After that thou shalt come to the hill of God, where *is* the garrison of the Philistines: and it shall come to pass, when thou art come thither to the city, that thou shalt meet a company of prophets coming down from the high place with a psaltery, and a tabret, and a pipe, and a harp, before them; and they shall prophesy:

And the Spirit of the LORD will come upon thee, and thou shalt prophesy with them, and shalt be turned into another man.

And it was *so*, that when he had turned his back to go from Samuel, God gave him another heart: and all those signs came to pass that day.

And when they came thither to the hill, behold, a company of prophets met him; and the Spirit of God came upon him, and he prophesied among them.

And it came to pass, when all that knew him beforetime saw that, behold, he prophesied among the prophets, then the people said one to another, What *is* this *that* is come unto the son of Kish? *Is* Saul also among the prophets?

1 Samuel 10:1-6, 9-11

The church needs an increased anointing as never before. This anointing will promote you and produce a new sense of direction for your life and ministry. Saul was not the same after his encounter with the prophetic anointing on the life of Samuel. He left with a prophetic word and a prophetic direction. He was turned into "another man." God gave him a "new heart." Saul wasn't prophesying when he started out, but he left prophesying among the bands of prophets. He came as a burden searcher, but left with the kingship anointing.

CHAPTER TWO

DISCERNING SPIRITUAL BRETHREN

The Body of Christ must know who spiritual brethren are and what makes a brother or sister spiritual. This lack of knowledge and understanding has caused an inaccurate operation and administration concerning the ways of God. The church has been ignorant and misinformed concerning spiritual brethren long enough. It is time for the church to wake up and realize that developing spiritual accuracy is dependent upon understanding spiritual brethren.

Discerning the Body

> Now about the spiritual gifts (the special endowments of supernatural energy), brethren, I do not want you to be misinformed.
>
> **1 Corinthians 12:1 AMP**

We have been taught many times that this is a chapter on the gifts of the Spirit. It is true that the various gifts of the Spirit are mentioned in this chapter, but that does not necessarily make it the gift chapter. This chapter is actually a chapter on the understanding and discerning of spiritual brethren.

We must realize, first of all, that the book of Corinthians actually deals with the church's learning and understanding regarding how to discern the Body of Christ. One of the greatest problems of the church today is the difficulty and the inability to discern the Body of Christ within their various groups and ministries. The lack of this discernment has been detrimental to the church. The church of God, in these last days, must quickly learn and understand how to discern the Body of Christ. In the book of Corinthians we also find the need for a cleansing of the church from false conceptions of the ministry, intellectual pride, social evils, and other disorders. It deals with strife concerning leadership and also with the true view of the ministry.

In the King James Version, it is written:

> Now concerning spiritual *gifts*, brethren, I would not have you ignorant.
>
> **1 Corinthians 12:1**

Notice that the word *gifts* is written in italics and not in the same lettering as the other words. This indicates that the word *gifts* was actually added later in this verse of Scripture to bring clarity and understanding. When the word *gifts* is taken out of this verse, the verse reads like this: *Now concerning spiritual brethren, I would not have you ignorant.*

It is very important that we fully understand this point: Paul was concerned about the state of spiritual brethren first, before the gifts. He was concerned about the lack of understanding and discerning of true spiritual brethren. Paul is actually telling the church not to be misinformed and unaware of who a spiritual brother or a spiritual sister is, while in their midst.

The question then is, how could Paul be talking about spiritual brethren and yet be talking about the gifts of the Spirit? Paul knew where to start. Most of us have been taught to start with the gifts and then move to the character development of the believer. But Paul, through the Holy Spirit, is showing the church the proper structure and order. We have been wrongly indoctrinated and, as a result, have put the cart before the ox. It is time now to put the ox first, before the cart!

The gifts of the Spirit do not operate in the air. The gifts of the Spirit operate through the lives of spiritual brothers and sisters. Most of our churches emphasize the operations of the gifts so greatly, which is good in the proper context. However, the gifts do not just operate on their own; rather, they operate through the lives of spiritual men and women.

We have become so "gift conscious" that we ignore the lifestyles of the individuals operating these gifts. The church will not be able to properly understand the manifestation, operation, and the administration of the gifts of the Spirit until she starts discerning and understanding who true spiritual brethren are within their midst.

The gifts of the Spirit are not just for one or two men within the church. They are for all of God's people who desire to operate in them. The problem is that for the manifestation, operation, and administration of the gifts to be accurate and believable today, the one being used in the gifts must possess the necessary lifestyle. He must be walking in some level of integrity and excellence. Many times in the church we see and hear men of wrong lifestyles operating in the gifts. Even though what they say may be correct, because these individuals are not walking right, the people listening become unable to confidently and accurately receive what they are saying. The knowledge of their lifestyle brings a level of devaluation to their message.

The danger of the lack of this understanding causes great inaccuracy in the operations of the gifts of the Spirit. We look for the gifts of the Spirit in operation and yet do not discern spiritual brethren. God is calling the church, first of all, to learn to discern spiritual brethren before the quest of the gifts. A person that is not spiritual will be inaccurate in his operation and will not be sharp in his administration; nor will he be able to pinpoint the movement, leading, and direction of God. They are but "spiritual guessers." They guess everything and are unable to fully understand the ways of God.

God does not want us to be unenlightened concerning true spiritual brethren in our midst. We must locate them. We must seek them out in our churches, groups, or organizations. And we must be willing to embrace these men and the anointing over their lives once they are recognized.

As the church begins to mark spiritual brethren in its midst, it will become much easier to detect an inaccurate word when it comes from a carnal minded believer. The lack of this detection is causing great problems in some churches today, as we see individuals who are carnal minded—not spiritual—giving words to people and claiming to operate in the Spirit.

We put great emphasis on the gifts without understanding and discerning the vessels that are used. There is nothing wrong in learning, understanding and operating in the gifts. But before this takes place, the Body of Christ must learn to discern and understand the vessels that God uses to operate these gifts.

Different Operation, Different Administration, and Different Manifestation

One operation is different from another. One manifestation and administration is different from another. Just because someone is not operating as you want, think, and have seen does not make them wrong as long as the operation and manifestation lines up with the Word of God. Spiritual brethren operate differently from one another. This does not make one wrong and the other right. Understanding spiritual brethren within your church, group, and congregation will allow you to be able to understand their operation, administration and manifestation, so that when such an individual begins to operate, it becomes much easier to understand, appreciate, and embrace the gift that is being released out of them.

A Novice

We have often witnessed men and women who have not been proven in the ways of God, who have risen up in churches and have declared "thus saith the Lord" without actually knowing how to hear from God. A lot of believers have been swayed and inaccurately directed because of such individuals. This is the hour in the history of the church that God is putting a demand on His leaders to discern and understand true spiritual brethren within their congregations.

I believe one of the main reasons for this is that along with the arrival of the downpouring of God's anointing comes the great need for spiritual accuracy and sharpness in its declaration and operation. The church is tired of men and women who, in the past, have inaccurately operated the gifts and were unable to locate the movement of the Spirit of God.

God will not allow the mistakes of the past to hinder His present movement. The days of inaccurate ministers and leaders operating in God's pulpits are gone. God is calling for accurate believers—those who are sharp in the ways of God and are able to detect and pinpoint the leading and direction of His Spirit.

Not Carried About by Dumb Idols

> You know that when you were heathen, you were led off after idols that could not speak [habitually] as impulse directed and whenever the occasion might arise.

1 Corinthians 12:2 AMP

Spiritual brethren are not carried about by dumb idols. They are not directed by their impulses. Instead, they are directed and controlled by the power of the Holy Ghost that abides inside of them. We have a lot of believers who are still controlled by their impulses and emotions. It is a dangerous thing to be controlled by your impulses and emotions, especially when it comes to the things of God.

A man or a woman who is directed and controlled by impulses cannot be accurate and sharp in the things of the Spirit. They cannot pinpoint what God is doing and saying. Many of these emotional and impulse-controlled Christians come before God's people and declare and decree the word of the Lord. Many stand in God's pulpits prophesying the word.

The reason they are still impulse directed is because they still allow themselves to be led and directed by the dumb idols that they were once delivered from. This is why God, through Paul, is admonishing the church not to be misinformed and unaware of spiritual brethren. The time of awareness and enlightenment has come.

The Characteristics of Spiritual Brethren

Therefore I want you to understand that no one speaking under the power and influence of the [Holy] Spirit of God can [ever] say, Jesus be cursed! And no one can [really] say, Jesus is [my] Lord, except by and under the power and influence of the Holy Spirit.

1 Corinthians 12:3 AMP

Here, Paul began to explain some of the qualities and characteristics of spiritual brethren. Spiritual brethren are always under the power and influence of the Holy Spirit. This means they are constantly and consistently being led by the Spirit of God. They cannot call Jesus, His Word or His practices accursed or abominable because they are under the influence of the Holy Spirit.

These brethren do not touch the accursed thing. The accursed thing is anything that is devoted to destruction. It could also be something consecrated to God that is taken by someone unlawfully. Men and women who are born again, tongue-talking, and blood-bought are consecrated to God. Anything outside the law and Word of God is unlawful.

Partaking and embracing such things puts you in the position of touching the accursed thing.

In the early church, it was a practice among the Jews to call Jesus "accursed," which in Greek is the word *anathema*— meaning one so abominable as to be unfit to live on earth. It was an early practice among the heathen persecutors to force believers to call Jesus accursed. Today, when a believer compromises and yields to the leading of the enemy, it is the same as one declaring that the power of God is unable to keep and protect. Most believers today call Jesus accursed by their behavior, actions, lifestyles, and their approach toward the Word of God.

True spiritual brethren will not, in their words, thoughts or deeds, call Jesus accursed. If they sin, they will immediately ask God for forgiveness and get back in fellowship with Him. They will not negate and declare Jesus' work on Calvary null and void.

The Manifestation of the Spirit

But the manifestation of the Spirit is given to every man to profit withal.

1 Corinthians 12:7

The evidence and the making visible of the Spirit have one purpose, and that is to *profit* the Body of Christ. But how can the body be profited from an inaccurate word? How can the body be profited from the spirit of one that calls Jesus accursed?

Men who are carnally minded, men who are not under the power and influence of the Holy Spirit, have manifested gifts whose evidence has caused great hurt to the Body, instead of profiting the Body. This is why it is paramount for the Body of Christ to be fully aware and understand who true spiritual brethren are.

Who Are Spiritual Brethren?

The Greek word for "spiritual" is *pneumatikon*. It refers to non-carnal, religious and spiritual things. The word brethren refers, actually, to members of a sect practicing the same "living" and "ways." It usually denotes "brotherhood." The early church members were called brethren because of how knitted together they were in the ways of God.

> For both he that sanctifieth and they who are sanctified *are* all of one: for which cause he is not ashamed to call them brethren,

> Hebrews 2:11

This Scripture explains it more clearly. Those who are sanctified, separated and made holy by God, who is the Sanctifier, have one Father and belong to one family. This makes us brethren, because we belong to one brotherhood in which God is the head of the brotherhood.

> For we know that the law is spiritual: but I am carnal, sold under sin.

> Romans 7:14

The commandment of God is not carnal, it is spiritual. If the Word of God is not carnal, then the men and women who walk and live according to the Word of God should not be carnal, but spiritual. Spiritual men and women are spiritually minded. They are totally concerned about the ways of the Spirit.

Carnal Brethren

Where there are spiritual men and women, there are also carnal men and women. The Greek word for "carnal" is *sarkikos,* which means to be fleshy, natural and human. Even though the spiritual man has flesh and blood, they are more than human. They operate on a higher dimension. The spiritual man lives and walks in the realm of the Spirit, while the carnal man does not. The spiritual man operates in the law of the Spirit of life in Christ Jesus, and is able to please God because he walks according to God's Word.

The carnal-minded Christian walks according to the law of sin and death. They walk according to the dictates of their emotions and impulses, and are in enmity with God because they mind the things of the flesh. Such an individual will not obey the law of God because they submit to sin. As long as the carnal believer lives in this rebellion, they cannot please God.

True Spirituality

True spirituality that produces accuracy is developed in three ways:

First, be open to biblical change. The Body of Christ must be ready and open to true biblical change. There are great changes going on today in the land and in the Body of Christ. There is the changing of the guards. There is a power change in the land. The baton is being exchanged from one hand to the other. The spirit of Saul is being dethroned and the house of David is being enthroned. A fresh and new Davidic dynasty is being installed. The glory of God is coming back home again! We must change with this flow of the Spirit of God. Anyone who will not change will have great difficulty coping in this hour.

Second, be committed to Jesus and His purpose. We must find the purpose of God for our lives and be totally committed to it. The reason most Christians are not committed today is because they have not been able to locate and understand the purpose of God for their lives. They are mixed up, confused, and unable to locate their place in the Body of Christ. Most believers think that they are just called to be born again and to sit down day and night without making a difference in the kingdom of the enemy. We must serve the purpose of God for our generation. Our generation is waiting for the time when the true sons of God will be manifested. Praise God we have true sons of God today! All we need is to find the purpose of God for our lives, lock in on it, and then begin to manifest it.

> **For David, after he had served his own generation by the will of God, fell on sleep, and was laid unto his fathers, and saw corruption:**
>
> **Acts 13:36**

Somewhere in time, David was able to discover the purpose, will and counsel of God for his destiny. After locating his purpose, the Bible says he "served" it until he "fell asleep." Note the word "served" in this Scripture. The only way to birth the purpose of God in our lives is by serving. We must be prepared to serve our generation. One reason why the purpose of God for our lives has not been fully manifested is because a lot of us do not want to serve.

Finally, we must learn to be adventurous with Christ Jesus and walk as Abraham did.

> By faith Abraham, when he was called to go out into a place which he should after receive for an inheritance, obeyed; and he went out, not knowing whither he went.
>
> By faith he sojourned in the land of promise, as *in* a strange country, dwelling in tabernacles with Isaac and Jacob, the heirs with him of the same promise:
>
> For he looked for a city which hath foundations, whose builder and maker *is* God.
>
> These all died in faith, not having received the promises, but having seen them afar off, and were persuaded of them, and embraced them, and confessed that they were strangers and pilgrims on the earth.
>
> **Hebrew 11:8-10,13**

Abraham walked by faith. When God told Abraham to move from where he was and go to another city, Abraham did not question God. He did not grumble and complain. He just obeyed God. He took God at His Word, knowing that God is true and faithful. He was ready to obey God twenty-four hours a day. We must also be flexible and ready to move when the orders are given.

Restoring a Brother or Sister

Not just any kind of Christian is to restore a fellow brother or sister. The Bible specifies the qualification of the restorer.

Brethren, if any person is overtaken in misconduct or sin of any sort, you who are spiritual [who are responsive to and controlled by the Spirit] should set him right and restore and reinstate him, without any sense of superiority and with all gentleness, keeping an attentive eye on yourself, lest you should be tempted also.

Galatians 6:1 AMP

The restorer must be spiritual! In other words, the person restoring an individual to his original state and condition must meet the criteria stated in the Word. We have a lot of Christians running around today trying to restore and reinstate other Christians from their overtaken faults, when in reality they inflict further damage to them. If you are not spiritual and do not meet the qualification stated in the Word of God, you do not have any business trying to restore someone else.

It is important that the restorer be spiritual, because true spiritual brethren possess certain qualities that carnal brethren do not. True spiritual brethren are controlled and responsive to the Spirit of God. They walk in the fruits of the Spirit.

However, brethren, I could not talk to you as to spiritual [men], but as to nonspiritual [men of the flesh, in whom the carnal nature predominates], as to mere infants [in the new life] in Christ

For you are still [unspiritual, having the nature] of the flesh [under the control of ordinary impulses]. For as long as [there are] envying and jealousy and wrangling and factions among you, are you not unspiritual and of the flesh, behaving yourselves after a human standard and like mere (unchanged) men?

For when one says, I belong to Paul, and another, I belong to Apollos, are you not [proving yourselves] ordinary (unchanged) men?

1 Corinthians 3:1, 3-4 AMP

Paul was able to distinguish the spiritual from the unspiritual brethren. He pinpointed some of the qualities of the unspiritual. We cannot claim to be spiritual if we are still operating and walking in jealousy, envy, divisions, and other works of the flesh. Operating in the works of the flesh puts the believers in the same category as mere men who walk after the human standard. Men or women that are born again and Holy Ghost filled are not mere men or women. They are different. Why? Because they have been translated into the Kingdom of God. We must see ourselves the way God sees us.

Locating Spiritual Brethren

Paul was one leader who was not playing church during his time. Within every church and city he entered, he made sure that he identified, discerned and located the true spiritual brothers and sisters within that church, group, or congregation.

But I hope in the Lord Jesus to send Timothy to you shortly, so that I also may be encouraged when I learn of your condition.

For I have no one else of kindred spirit who will genuinely be concerned for your welfare.

For they all seek after their own interests, not

those of Christ Jesus.

But you know of his proven worth, that he
served with me in the furtherance of the gospel
like a child serving his father.

Philippians 2:19-22 NASB

In writing to the church at Philippi, Paul was able to locate and identify Timothy as a spiritual brother. He talked about Timothy as one having a kindred spirit. It is very difficult today to find men and women that have this kind of Spirit. Thank God that the apostolic reformation in this hour is birthing men of kindred spirit. This is a very powerful quality that God's people must possess in this hour. A person with a kindred spirit is like-minded to the vision of the house and the leader. They possess the same "family mentality" to accomplish the purposes of God.

Showing Your Worth

But you know of his proven worth, that he
served with me in the furtherance of the gospel
like a child serving his father.

Philippians 2:22 NASB

Your worth must be proven to be recognized as a true spiritual brother. Many Christians want to lead and be in various positions, yet they have not been proven. Your worth must be proven in order to be known and appreciated. Your walk, your lifestyle, your submission, your commitment, your dedication, and your persistence in the things of God will help to prove your worth. Paul talked about the proven worth of Timothy. Your worth must be known and appreciated by others first. Note carefully how Timothy's worth was proven.

It was through his acts of serving. We must prove our worth by serving the purpose of God.

Note what Paul said in verse 22, "But you know of his *proven worth* that he served." The church at Philippi knew Timothy's worth. They knew Paul was not just making up a nice story about Timothy, but was speaking about something that was true. The church at Philippi knew that Timothy's worth was proven through serving them. This is how our worth should be proven today. It should be by serving God's people faithfully and truthfully.

The knowledge of Timothy's own worth enabled the people to embrace him and what he had to say without any doubt in their minds concerning his spiritual position. They already knew he was a spiritual brother by his service and his style of life. His words were not questioned by the church. His giftings were not doubtful or even questionable in the minds of the people, because he had been proven faithful. This is what it is all about when understanding true and faithful brethren.

There are a lot of Christians that operate with dark clouds over their lives and ministries. Their operations are questionable because their lifestyle, commitment, and dedication to the *Way* does not match the gift they are operating in. They talk the gift, but do not walk in the way of the gift.

Being Profitable and Begotten

I appeal to you for my child Onesimus, whom I have begotten in my imprisonment,

who formerly was useless to you, but now is useful both to you and to me.
I have sent him back to you in person, that is, sending my very heart,

whom I wished to keep with me, so that on your behalf he might minister to me in my imprisonment for the gospel;

but without your consent I did not want to do anything, so that your goodness would not be, in effect, by compulsion but of your own free will.

For perhaps he was for this reason separated from you for a while, that you would have him back forever,

no longer as a slave, but more than a slave, a beloved brother, especially to me, but how much more to you, both in the flesh and in the Lord.

If then you regard me a partner, accept him as you would me.

Philemon 10-17 NASB

Paul, in writing to his friend Philemon, located another spiritual brother. He identified Onesimus as a profitable and useful brother. Onesimus was described by Paul as once being *unprofitable*. In other words, there was a time he was not a spiritual brother. There were times he did not walk and operate according to the laws of God. There were times when his lifestyle did not match the words he spoke. This applies to us today. We have a lot of Christians that are still unprofitable to their call, church, ministry and group because of their lifestyles.

Interestingly, Paul knew about the change in the life of Onesimus. He wanted the church to know that Onesimus was a changed man. He wanted the church to know that Onesimus was now a spiritual brother. He interceded on behalf of Onesimus. Unprofitable men and women cannot be accurate with the ways of God. The church had to know that Onesimus had become useful and therefore profitable. Paul was able to discern the profitability of Onesimus. He knew when Onesimus was useless and when he became profitable!

Fellow Bond Servants

> All my state shall Tychicus declare unto you, *who is* a beloved brother, and a faithful minister and fellowservant in the Lord:
>
> Whom I have sent unto you for the same purpose, that he might know your estate, and comfort your hearts;
>
> And Jesus, which is called Justus, who are of the circumcision. These only *are my* fellowworkers unto the kingdom of God, which have been a comfort unto me.
>
> Epaphras, who is *one* of you, a servant of Christ, saluteth you, always labouring fervently for you in prayers, that ye may stand perfect and complete in all the will of God.
>
> For I bear him record, that he hath a great zeal for you, and them *that are* in Laodicea, and them in Hierapolis.
>
> Colossians 4:7-8,11-13

Paul again identified and located his fellow workers. He spoke of them as spiritual brethren and proclaimed their faithfulness, commitment and dedication. He identified their individual roles and how they had been profitable to him.

The Household of Stephanas and Fortunatus

I beseech you, brethren, (ye know the house of Stephanas, that it is the firstfruits of Achaia, and that they have addicted themselves to the ministry of the saints,)

That ye submit yourselves unto such, and to every one that helpeth with us, and laboureth.

I am glad of the coming of Stephanas and Fortunatus and Achaicus: for that which was lacking on your part they have supplied.

For they have refreshed my spirit and yours: therefore acknowledge ye them that are such.

1 Corinthians 16:15-18

The house of Stephanas and Fortunatus were identified as spiritual brethren. Paul spoke of them as the "firstfruits of Achaia," and spoke of their devotion to the ministry. He made a very significant statement in describing them. He spoke of them as being *addicted to the ministry of the saints.* Our addictions and passions must be towards Him and His work. We must be addicted to the ways of the Lord. The work of God must be paramount in our hearts.

Paul said that the house of Stephanas and Fortunatus had *supplied what was lacking* and *have refreshed my spirit.* This is a beautiful portrait of spiritual brethren. Spiritual brethren help their leaders, their churches, ministries and organizations by supplying what is lacking and by refreshing the spirit of all of those they are in contact with.

CHAPTER THREE

FLOWING WITH THE CHANGE
OF THE SPIRIT OF GOD

Accuracy involves making changes and adjustments in our lives. There are changes going on in the spirit realm within the Body of Christ. There is a new reformation of the Spirit of God. The old house is being destroyed and a new house is being rebuilt. Leaders and ministry gifts are being changed. God is shifting His power and favor from the house of Saul to the house of David! Illegal gods are being dethroned. The Body of Christ is experiencing the changing of the guard. A new Davidic dynasty is being installed. The Tabernacle of David is being restored. The Ark of God (which represents the presence and glory of God) is coming back home. It is coming to where it actually belongs. The ark has remained in Kiriath-jearim too long (the city of woods). It is time for it to be brought back to the city of Zion. Hallelujah! The Spirit of God is doing away with old styles, mechanisms, and cultures. Instead, God is raising men and women who are accurate, sharp, and can pinpoint the very movement and direction of God today.

Following the Due Order

**And they set the ark of God upon a new cart,
and brought it out of the house of Abinadab**

that *was* in Gibeah: and Uzzah and Ahio, the
sons of Abinadab, drave the new cart.

And they brought it out of the house of
Abinadab which *was* at Gibeah, accompanying
the ark of God: and Ahio went before the ark.

And David and all the house of Israel played
before the LORD on all manner of *instruments
made of* fir wood, even on harps, and on
psalteries, and on timbrels, and on cornets, and
on cymbals.

And when they came to Nachon's
threshingfloor, Uzzah put forth *his hand* to the
ark of God, and took hold of it; for the oxen
shook *it.*

And the anger of the LORD was kindled against
Uzzah; and God smote him there for *his* error;
and there he died by the ark of God.

2 Samuel 6:3-7

Looking at the above Scriptures, you can see the operation
of the old move and why a change is mandatory. David put
the Ark of the Covenant on a new cart pulled by oxen to bring
it back to Jerusalem. At one point, the oxen stumbled and
Uzzah stretched forth his hand to steady the tottering Ark.
God struck Uzzah dead for his rash act. Often believers are
concerned with why God dealt so harshly with Uzzah.

Notice in verse 3 that Uzzah was one of the sons of
Abinadab. The Ark had been kept in the house of Abinadab
for twenty years. Uzzah had grown up in a house where the
Ark, the glory, and the presence of God were part of the
everyday furniture. The Ark had become so familiar to him
that it lost its significance, and he lost his sense of reverence

toward it. Therefore, he became presumptuous, stretching out the arm of flesh in order to help God out.

So often there is the danger, especially with the generations of Christians and leaders who have experienced the various movements of God, to develop a familiarity with the ways of God. They limit their expectations of what God will do, and they fail to press into God. They start relying on the arm of flesh and fall flat on their faces, as Uzzah did. The Body of Christ today must learn a great lesson from the experience of Uzzah. In Hebrew ,"Uzzah" is a name which means "strength." Uzzah represents the natural strength of man and reliance on man's might, instead of God's.

Note that David and his men failed in their first attempt to bring back the Ark — the glory, and the presence of God — because they tried to follow the Philistine pattern. They treated the Ark with too much familiarity, and failed to give it the reverence it deserved by relying on their own strength and understanding.

This is why the church has been in jeopardy from one movement to the other. Men and women in the Body of Christ treated the change, the movement, and the arrival of the Holy Spirit with familiarity and without due reverence. This lack has caused inaccuracies with the manifestations of the Spirit of God through the lives of most believers, and also with the operation and the administration of the gifts.

Many Christians have remained where God used to be. They don't realize God is no longer there. It is true that God used to be there, but He is no longer there. What happens is that these individuals operate in the style and mechanism of the old movement. They fail to understand that God has moved somewhere else now. It is very dangerous to remain where God used to be. We must learn to flow with the Spirit of God. We must go where He goes and do what He instructs us to do. The church must be flexible to change with any movement of God, and not to remain starchy and rigid in our old traditional ways and styles.

What is Change?

The word "change" means to alter a pattern. It means to exchange for, or to replace by another. It also means to put fresh clothes and covering on. It means to substitute and abandon for another thing. It could also mean to transfer from one train to another.

This brings clarity to what is happening today and helps to explain the change going on throughout the land. God, through His Spirit, is altering the old regime and its pattern. The Spirit of God is altering all codes and protocol toward a new one. There is a spiritual coup d'etat going on in Christendom. The Spirit of God is exchanging and replacing old leaders, old ways, old mechanisms and old starchy styles for new ones. God is transferring men and women from one reformation train to another. God is calling and demanding that His people flow with the change.

> Thus saith the LORD of hosts, I remember *that* which Amalek did to Israel, how he laid *wait* for him in the way, when he came up from Egypt.
>
> Now go and smite Amalek, and utterly destroy all that they have, and spare them not; but slay both man and woman, infant and suckling, ox and sheep, camel and ass.

And he took Agag the king of the Amalekites alive, and utterly destroyed all the people with the edge of the sword.

But Saul and the people spared Agag, and the best of the sheep, and of the oxen, and of the fatlings, and the lambs, and all *that was* good, and would not utterly destroy them: but every thing *that was* vile and refuse, that they destroyed utterly.

And Saul said, They have brought them from the Amalekites: for the people spared the best of the sheep and of the oxen, to sacrifice unto the LORD thy God; and the rest we have utterly destroyed.

Then Samuel said unto Saul, Stay, and I will tell thee what the LORD hath said to me this night. And he said unto him, Say on.

And Samuel said unto Saul, I will not return with thee: for thou hast rejected the word of the LORD, and the LORD hath rejected thee from being king over Israel.

And as Samuel turned about to go away, he laid hold upon the skirt of his mantle, and it rent.

And Samuel said unto him, The LORD hath rent the kingdom of Israel from thee this day, and hath given it to a neighbour of thine, *that is* better than thou.

1 Samuel 15:2-3, 8-9, 15-16, 26-28

This is an example of an individual and a leader who would not flow with the change. Change may not be easy, but change is possible. King Saul was specifically instructed by God through the prophet Samuel to go and completely destroy the Amalekites in retribution for what they did to the Israelites on their way to the Promised Land. Change will always come with a purpose. Going to battle and destroying the enemy was not new to Saul and his armies, nor to any king of Israel. The pattern of the battle and the aftermath of it were Saul's concern and problem. King Saul was used to the old pattern of battle and its aftermath of rewards.

He was accustomed to the old pattern of a king or a leader automatically taking the spoils of the enemy, once that enemy was completely and successfully defeated. King Saul and his armies were already used to this mode of operation. The king and his armies selected the best of everything and gathered for themselves the spoils of their enemies. Therefore, it was strange and new to Saul and his armies to completely destroy the Amalekites without taking any of the spoils of war.

Even though Saul had agreed to completely obey the Lord's instructions, he was neither ready nor able to flow with the new change. A man who is truly ready to change will resist any negative counsel from the enemy that would prevent him from changing. Saul was easily persuaded not to change by the same people who God had instructed him to destroy. He forgot the word of the Lord given to him by the prophet. He obeyed the words and advice of the enemy that kept him in the old style and pattern. Change is not just in words, change has to do with actions and lifestyles.

King Saul went to the Amalek battle with the same old mind set. He refused to flow with the change, whether it was a temporal change or a permanent change. He went into battle operating with the same old strategy. He and his armies killed all they wished to kill, and then took the best of everything. We have leaders and believers who are just like

Saul and his armies today. They will not flow with the change and the movement of the Holy Spirit, nor will they allow their congregation to flow with it either.

They (Saul and company) preferred the old style, the old way, the old equipment, the old tradition and the old pattern. It is dangerous to go by the old when the new is available. Sooner or later, the old will run out of spare parts.

The Prophetic Confrontation

> And Samuel came to Saul: and Saul said unto him, Blessed *be* thou of the LORD: I have performed the commandment of the LORD.
>
> And Samuel said, What *meaneth* then this bleating of the sheep in mine ears, and the lowing of the oxen which I hear?
>
> And Saul said, They have brought them from the Amalekites: for the people spared the best of the sheep and of the oxen, to sacrifice unto the LORD thy God; and the rest we have utterly destroyed.
>
> 1 Samuel 15:13-15

The prophetic anointing will attack and confront sin in this hour. Saul was confronted by the prophet Samuel concerning his lack of obedience to God. Change demands obedience. The apostolic and the prophetic anointing is available in this hour to confront men and leaders who will not flow with the change and movement of the Spirit of God. The prophet Samuel confronted Saul not just because he took the best of the spoils and spared the king. After all, that was not unusual for a king and his armies to do after successfully defeating its enemies. Samuel confronted him because he had disobeyed

God and had failed to change to what God demanded out of Amalek. Saul failed to flow with the change, because it was different than the pattern of operation during previous battles executed by him and his predecessors.

No Excuse

> **And Saul said, They have brought them from the Amalekites: for the people spared the best of the sheep and of the oxen, to sacrifice unto the LORD thy God; and the rest we have utterly destroyed.**
>
> **1 Samuel 15:15**

When God demands a change, He means a change. God does not need any excuses for lack of change. This was exactly what Saul was doing. He was giving the prophet an excuse for not obeying and flowing with the change of God. We have a lot of folks in the Body of Christ who will make up various excuses not to change. "This is how my pastor does it," or, "We have been doing it this way for 20 years," are some of our excuses. This was what Saul was doing. He was giving reasons why he did not obey God.

Refusal to Change

> **For rebellion *is as* the sin of witchcraft, and stubbornness *is as* iniquity and idolatry. Because thou hast rejected the word of the LORD, he hath also rejected thee from *being* king.**
>
> **And Saul said unto Samuel, I have sinned: for I have transgressed the commandment of the LORD, and thy words: because I feared the people, and obeyed their voice.**

Now therefore, I pray thee, pardon my sin, and turn again with me, that I may worship the LORD.

And Samuel said unto Saul, I will not return with thee: for thou hast rejected the word of the LORD, and the LORD hath rejected thee from being king over Israel.

And as Samuel turned about to go away, he laid hold upon the skirt of his mantle, and it rent.

And Samuel said unto him, The LORD hath rent the kingdom of Israel from thee this day, and hath given it to a neighbour of thine, *that is* better than thou.

1 Samuel 15:23-28

The reward and repercussion of not changing is very disastrous and devastating. Saul's refusal to obey God and flow with the change cost him his anointing, his call, and his kingdom. The baton was immediately transferred in the spirit realm to someone else who was willing and flexible to flow with the change.

When the favor, the glory, and the Spirit of God leaves an individual, he or she is on their own. The individual is like an empty shell. Saul was on his own. He was a king without a kingdom, without an anointing or the favor of God. Likewise, we have leaders in charge of churches and ministries without the favor, the glory, and the anointing of God to rule or govern, because it has been rent away from them. These individuals still lead God's people and claim to operate in the Spirit. What they are simply doing is operating in the old way and pattern, with the old methods.

Flowing with the change of the Spirit will birth the spirit of accuracy. An individual that does not flow with change is never accurate in his season. They operate with the tools, ways, and styles of old. They are not current with the new ways of God. Their modes of operation are outdated. They talk about the past and its operation.

Christians who consistently sit under the ministries of these individuals also become inaccurate in the ways of God. They become indoctrinated and instilled with the mentality of the old when the new arrives. They are trained, mentored, and developed with the old wineskin.

Exchanging the Javelin

The church is seeing the exchange of the javelin as never before. Men and women are being constrained by the Spirit of God to turn over power to others. It is not being done nor achieved by violent means, nor by any works of the flesh. But God, through His Spirit, is convincing men and women who will not change to step down the ladder for those who will flow with His change. Whether voluntarily or involuntarily, the baton is being exchanged.

> And the women answered *one another* as they played, and said, Saul hath slain his thousands, and David his ten thousands.
>
> And Saul was very wroth, and the saying displeased him; and he said, They have ascribed unto David ten thousands, and to me they have ascribed *but* thousands: and *what* can he have more but the kingdom?
>
> And Saul eyed David from that day and forward.

> **And it came to pass on the morrow, that the evil spirit from God came upon Saul, and he prophesied in the midst of the house: and David played with his hand, as at other times: and *there was* a javelin in Saul's hand.**
>
> **And Saul cast the javelin; for he said, I will smite David even to the wall *with it*. And David avoided out of his presence twice.**
>
> **And Saul was afraid of David, because the LORD was with him, and was departed from Saul.**

1 Samuel 18:7-12

The javelin represented the staff of power and authority. In the western part of Africa, especially in Nigeria and among the Itsekiri clan, the javelin plays a great role in the coronation ceremony of a king. The coronation of a king is never complete until the javelin, which is the staff of power, is turned over from the old king, whether dead or alive, to the new king.

The individual may be adorned in full regal attire, with the king's crown, robes, shoes, and other regalia, but if there is no staff of power, that individual is a king without any power and authority. The javelin is usually the last tool or piece of equipment that is given or turned over to the individual after his coronation as king. So, we can see the importance and symbolism of the javelin. In the Old Testament, the javelin also played a great role in the coronation process.

Saul's throwing or casting of the javelin at David, with the intention to kill him, symbolically denotes the exchange of power. Even though Saul himself did not realize this, he was actually turning over the staff of power to David. He was turning over power unknowingly and involuntarily. The church will see this exchange more often in this movement of the Spirit of God. Situations and intentions born in evil will receive automatic change for the good.

Ministers will unconsciously turn over their power, their domain and their self-made kingdoms to other men and women who have been called, ordained, and held with the favor and anointing of God upon their lives.

When Saul threw the javelin to kill David, little did he realize that what he was doing was actually turning over his power to the man that God had ordained for the hour. Churches and ministers that are not flowing with the change will experience great drought and famine.

Symptoms of Change

Change has certain symptoms that must be quickly detected. A symptom is a functional condition that actually indicates the presence of a thing. It is the sign that serves to point out the existence of something else. The symptoms help and aid in the diagnosis of the cause of an entity.

An individual detects that a certain allergy or sickness is coming upon him or her because of the symptoms produced by that allergy or sickness. When a negative symptom is not attended to, it transforms itself into the actual disease and might kill the individual. Change has its own symptoms. These symptoms must be quickly detected and properly responded to.

Most Christians do not change because they do not know or understand the *symptoms* of change, nor how to respond to them. Some Christians realize these symptoms but will do nothing about it.

The most important symptom of change is *frustration*. Frustration is when an individual is completely disappointed in or by something and thwarted by it. The frustration can be in regard to an individual and his or her acts. It can be about a church or a ministry. It can be over a particular doctrine and teaching of a church or of an individual. It can be over certain man-made traditional acts, behaviors, and protocols that do not line up with the Word of God. It can even be over a personal habit which has been very difficult to eradicate.

Kinds of Frustration

There are godly frustrations and ungodly frustrations. We have been taught that frustration is a sin and that when a person gets frustrated they are not spiritual. Do you know or realize that there has never been a change, from generations until now, that has not been birthed from frustration? All changes, known and unknown, has been the product of frustration, whether they are spiritual changes or physical changes. Both individual and corporate changes have all been birthed from some form of frustration.

This prophetic movement of the Spirit of God will produce frustration in the lives of Christian leaders, churches, and ministries who desire to change. They will no longer be satisfied and comfortable with their tradition and starchy ways. They will not be satisfied with that old style of ministering and the old dry style of worshipping without the presence of the anointing. They will seek for where they can be fed. They will seek for where the anointing is visible and in full operation and will cry for justice to flow in their churches and in their land like a river, and righteousness like an overflowing stream.

They will desire a change in their lives, in their churches and in their ministries. They will fight for change. They will bombard heaven with prayer and fasting for a new outpouring and a new refreshing upon their lives, their leaders, their churches, and their ministries. They will move with the cloud. It is happening right now. Watch out church, the change has begun!

Godly Frustration

A godly or positive frustration is one that has both a *cause* and *energy.* Many Christians are frustrated and disappointed, but their frustration or disappointment has no *cause,* and therefore no *energy.*

Ungodly Frustration

An ungodly or negative frustration is one that has no cause or energy. A positive or godly cause will produce the appropriate energy to accomplish the purpose of the frustration. But a negative or ungodly cause will produce no energy. We have examples of people who just don't like a thing, or who are disappointed with their leaders, churches, fellow members, their jobs, their relationships and even their families without a cause. They just get frustrated because they see and hear someone else being disappointed. If you ask them the cause of their frustration they will not be able to tell you.

We have Christians who are just frustrated with their leaders because they do not share the same opinions. If you ask such individuals what is the cause of their frustration, they will not be able to tell you exactly. Your frustration must be godly. It must have a godly cause and it must not be a selfish cause. A frustration with an ungodly cause will not possess the energy to execute its purpose. We have folks who talk about change, but they do not possess the energy to change because they do not have a godly frustration with a godly cause.

Cause

The *cause* is the rational ground for your action and choice. It is the ever-burning reason and desire for your action. Your "rational ground" and reason must be scriptural.

Energy

The *energy* is the force and power that enables an effective execution of the cause without the normally attendant fatigue. The *energy* is the anointing that quickens the individual to fulfill the *cause* of the frustration. Both the cause and the energy are spirit-injected. It cannot be artificial. If it is artificial, then that frustration is not godly. It must be genuine and sincere. It has to do with the heart, and not with the emotions and impulses.

Let's look at the following Scriptures carefully:

> Now the Philistines gathered together their armies to battle, and were gathered together at Shochoh, which *belongeth* to Judah, and pitched between Shochoh and Azekah, in Ephesdammim.

And Saul and the men of Israel were gathered together, and pitched by the valley of Elah, and set the battle in array against the Philistines.

And the Philistines stood on a mountain on the one side, and Israel stood on a mountain on the other side: and *there was* a valley between them.

And there went out a champion out of the camp of the Philistines, named Goliath, of Gath, whose height *was* six cubits and a span.

And *he had* an helmet of brass upon his head, and he *was* armed with a coat of mail; and the weight of the coat *was* five thousand shekels of brass.

And *he had* greaves of brass upon his legs, and a target of brass between his shoulders.

And the staff of his spear *was* like a weaver's beam; and his spear's head *weighed* six hundred shekels of iron: and one bearing a shield went before him.

And he stood and cried unto the armies of Israel, and said unto them, Why are ye come out to set *your* battle in array? *am* not I a Philistine, and ye servants to Saul? choose you a man for you, and let him come down to me.

If he be able to fight with me, and to kill me, then will we be your servants: but if I prevail against him, and kill him, then shall ye be our servants, and serve us.

And the Philistine said, I defy the armies of Israel this day; give me a man, that we may fight together.

When Saul and all Israel heard those words of the Philistine, they were dismayed, and greatly afraid.

Now David *was* the son of that Ephrathite of Bethlehemjudah, whose name *was* Jesse; and he had eight sons: and the man went among men *for* an old man in the days of Saul.

And Jesse said unto David his son, Take now for thy brethren an ephah of this parched *corn*, and these ten loaves, and run to the camp to thy brethren;

And carry these ten cheeses unto the captain of *their* thousand, and look how thy brethren fare, and take their pledge.

And David rose up early in the morning, and left the sheep with a keeper, and took, and went, as Jesse had commanded him; and he came to the trench, as the host was going forth to the fight, and shouted for the battle.

And David left his carriage in the hand of the keeper of the carriage, and ran into the army, and came and saluted his brethren.

And as he talked with them, behold, there came up the champion, the Philistine of Gath, Goliath by name, out of the armies of the Philistines, and spake according to the same words: and David heard *them*.

And David spake to the men that stood by him, saying, What shall be done to the man that killeth this Philistine, and taketh away the reproach from Israel? for who *is* this uncircumcised Philistine, that he should defy the armies of the living God?

And Eliab his eldest brother heard when he spake unto the men; and Eliab's anger was kindled against David, and he said, Why camest thou down hither? and with whom hast thou left those few sheep in the wilderness? I know thy pride, and the naughtiness of thine heart; for thou art come down that thou mightest see the battle.

And David said, What have I now done? *Is there* not a cause?

And David said to Saul, Let no man's heart fail because of him; thy servant will go and fight with this Philistine.

And Saul said to David, Thou art not able to go against this Philistine to fight with him: for thou *art but* a youth, and he a man of war from his youth.

And David said unto Saul, Thy servant kept his father's sheep, and there came a lion, and a bear, and took a lamb out of the flock:

And I went out after him, and smote him, and delivered *it* out of his mouth: and when he arose against me, I caught *him* by his beard, and smote him, and slew him.

1 Samuel 17:1-12,17-18,20,22,23-26,28-29,32-35

I would like you to carefully flow with me as we begin to examine these Scriptures. At this time, the Israelites were preparing for battle against the Philistines. The difference between this battle and other battles and wars fought by the Israelites was that, instead of the Israelite armies fighting corporately against the Philistine armies, the Philistines through Goliath of Gath requested and demanded an individual battle.

Goliath wanted the Israelites to choose a man from among them that would fight him. Even though the choice seemed simple for the Philistines, the choice was very difficult for the Israelites. The Israelites, from the king down to the armies, were afraid and dismayed. They had no one who would go against Goliath. They had no immediate choice.

David, on an errand from his father Jesse, appeared on the scene. God always knows the right time to put certain people on the scene for specific purposes. I believe that it was a spiritual set-up for a spiritual victory. David heard Goliath taunting the armies of Israel and saw how afraid the armies were. He was *frustrated*—disappointed over the entire situation. He was upset that the Philistines were defying the armies of the living God.

You see, David's disappointment or frustration had a *cause*. The cause was that Goliath was defying, humiliating, and embarrassing the armies of the living God. David was not concerned about himself. He was more concerned with the reproach brought on by Goliath's defiance of the armies of Israel. This cause burned like fire in David's veins. It produced a corresponding energy. David began to inquire more about what would be done for the person or man that defeated Goliath.

Note carefully that David's main cause was that Goliath defied the armies of the living God. But as he began to receive more feedback concerning the reward of the person that would defeat Goliath, David's cause began to increase. It increased from the defiance of God's armies to the desire of making his father's house free in Israel, being enriched with great riches and being married to the king's daughter. All of these causes compounded to create the energy to accomplish the job.

Look at David's reply to his eldest brother Eliab in verse 29. Eliab was angry and jealous of David. He thought David was proud because he was asking about the war and getting disappointed about the entire situation. Most times when you are disappointed over a situation and demand a change, there are some Christians and even ministers who might think you are proud, cocky, and unsubmissive to authority.

But David's reply to his brother was, "Is there not a cause?" In other words, he was telling his brother that he was not just being proud or cocky, but that he had rational ground for his action and choice. His frustration or disappointment birthed a cause. The cause or the rational ground was the fact that the army of the living God was being defied.

Whenever there is a godly cause, there is always a corresponding energy to accomplish it. The energy, which is the anointing of the Holy Spirit, comes from the presence of God. The cause of the frustration cannot be accomplished by man's devices, strategies, or tactics. It cannot be accomplished by man's tools or equipment. It can only be achieved by the Spirit of the living God. It takes the anointing to defeat the Goliaths in your life, not just some man-made tactics, devices, or strategies. The result of the battle was a foregone conclusion! The end was victory for the Israelite armies and a promotion for David.

The second symptom of change is the feeling of being resisted, useless, and unsatisfied. Many Christians experience this constantly. There are ministries and churches that are so rigidly established that no Spirit-inspired ideas or suggestions can be received. They have strong traditional protocols that do not permit new ideas. Many Christians in these kinds of groups, churches, and ministries begin to feel resisted and useless. It is true that not every idea or suggestion needs to be accepted, but there is a need for spiritual flexibility so that when the Spirit of God brings an idea through an individual, it can be properly discerned to see whether it is true or not.

Many times when you are resisted over something that is God ordained, inspired and directed, know that change is about to come. To be resisted means to fight or struggle against an individual idea, dream, vision or call, or seeking to foil an individual idea, dream, vision or call.

> And Ahab told Jezebel all that Elijah had done, and withal how he had slain all the prophets with the sword.
>
> Then Jezebel sent a messenger unto Elijah, saying, So let the gods do *to me*, and more also, if I make not thy life as the life of one of them by to morrow about this time.
>
> And when he saw *that*, he arose, and went for his life, and came to Beersheba, which *belongeth* to Judah, and left his servant there.
>
> But he himself went a day's journey into the wilderness, and came and sat down under a juniper tree: and he requested for himself that he might die; and said, It is enough; now, O LORD, take away my life; for I *am* not better than my fathers.

1 Kings 19:1-4

Elijah had this same feeling. He felt resisted by Ahab and Jezebel. His God-given reformation was met with great resistance from the King Ahab and his wife Jezebel. They fought against the spiritual cleansing that was needed in the land. They fought against the removal of false gods, false prophets and false styles of worship. They fought against the removal of apostasy. This produced great resistance to Elijah. He felt useless. He requested to die. This does not sound like a statement from a person that is comfortable and accepted. This sounds like words from a person that has been resisted and feels useless.

Elijah did not care if he was dead. This is pretty serious, especially from the mouth of a prophet. We have many Christians, and even leaders, in this same predicament. They get so resisted by their deacons, their church boards, their congregations, and even fellow ministers, that they begin to develop negative feelings about themselves, their callings, and their ministries. Some even quit their churches and ministries.

Elijah's resistance began to make him complain and murmur. He complained about Israel's forsaking of God's covenant, the throwing down of God's altars, and the slaying of God's prophets. Many times, when a Christian is wrongly resisted, that individual finds himself in a complaining mood. He or she becomes a complaining fanatic. God does not like His people to complain or murmur against leadership and against the authority of the house.

> **And the LORD said unto him, Go, return on thy way to the wilderness of Damascus: and when thou comest, anoint Hazael *to be* king over Syria:**
>
> **And Jehu the son of Nimshi shalt thou anoint *to be* king over Israel: and Elisha the son of**

Shaphat of Abelmeholah shalt thou anoint *to be* prophet in thy room.

And it shall come to pass, that him that escapeth the sword of Hazael shall Jehu slay: and him that escapeth from the sword of Jehu shall Elisha slay.

1 Kings 19:15-17

Did you notice that God did not address Elijah's complaint? He was concerned about the change that was to take place. While Elijah was busy complaining, God was preparing for a change in the land. Instead of complaining, let us flow with the change. We have the symptoms. It is now time to change. Stop the complaining, grumbling, and murmuring. Just change. The church of God must be prepared to flow with the change that the Holy Spirit is initiating throughout the land.

God was about to change the house of Ahab and replace it with the house of Jehu. God instructed Elijah to go to Damascus and anoint Hazael to be king over Syria and Jehu to be king over Israel, with Elisha to be prophet in Elijah's stead. Notice the three changes that God was initiating in Israel. The house of Ahab was to be changed to the house of Jehu. The house of Ben-hadad, king of Syria, was to be changed to the house of Hazael. Elisha the prophet was to be raised up in the stead of Elijah. A new prophetic anointing was to come over the land. The change was not only for the children of Israel, but also for the neighboring state (Syria). A fresh, new prophetic anointing was to be initiated in the land.

The Single-Portion Anointing Versus the Double-Portion Anointing

The prophet Elisha was a type or a representation of the double-portion reign of the Spirit of God. God was to restore back a double portion of His anointing upon His people Israel.

There was a difference between the anointing on the life of Elijah and that of Elisha. The prophet Elijah was a proclaimer and a carrier of a single portion of God's anointing, while Elisha was to be a carrier of a double portion of God's anointing. God was actually changing from the single-portion anointing to the double-portion anointing, by the prophet Elijah's anointing of Elisha.

> The glory of this latter house shall be greater than of the former, saith the LORD of hosts: and in this place will I give peace, saith the LORD of hosts.
>
> **Haggai 2:9**

God is doing exactly the same thing today. The church is actually undergoing a change from the former house to the glory of the latter house. There is a change from the single-portion anointing to the double-portion anointing. God is raising up men and women in this end time that will operate on a higher dimension than before. God is raising up ministers and leaders that will be carriers of this double-portion anointing.

We still have those who are satisfied with the single–portion anointing upon their lives, their churches and their lands. The church must realize that only the double portion of God's anointing will get men and women changed today. Most Christians have been used to the single-portion anointing. Now it is time for the double portion of God's anointing to encompass our churches, our lives, and our lands.

The Body of Christ needs this double-portion anointing to cause dead bones in our pews and pulpits to live again, and to cause fire to burn afresh in our bones. God knew that the double-portion anointing would change the land. Although God was not immediately replacing Elijah with Elisha, He was preparing the arrival of the double-portion anointing that would be pioneered by the prophet Elisha.

> And Elisha saw *it*, and he cried, My father, my father, the chariot of Israel, and the horsemen thereof. And he saw him no more: and he took hold of his own clothes, and rent them in two pieces.
>
> He took up also the mantle of Elijah that fell from him, and went back, and stood by the bank of Jordan;
>
> And he took the mantle of Elijah that fell from him, and smote the waters, and said, Where *is* the LORD God of Elijah? and when he also had smitten the waters, they parted hither and thither: and Elisha went over.
>
> **2 Kings 2:12-14**

After the departure of the prophet Elijah, who was a type of the single-portion anointing, came the arrival of the double-portion anointing on the life of the prophet Elisha. The prophet Elisha pioneered the arrival, the acceptance, and the operation of the double-portion anointing. The prophet Elisha was used mightily by God and wrought more miracles in his time than any other prophet, except Moses. This is exactly what is about to happen to the church of God in this end time movement of the Spirit of God. As believers, ministers and leaders, let go of the movement of the past with its tools, equipment, starchy styles of operations and mechanisms. God will cause the arrival, the acceptance, and the operation of the double-portion anointing to come upon His church.

The single-portion anointing was good. But the church needs the double-portion anointing. The double-portion anointing will cause the land to be fertile again. It will cause a resurrection of the prophetic. It will bring back the focus, dependence, reliance, trust, commitment, and total dedication of the church to its Maker. It will bring back the spirit of accuracy and pinpointing. This double-portion anointing will cause men and women to be saved without great effort. It will restore the fear of the Lord and will bring back the Ark of the Lord to its original place.

Which Bank of the River Are You On— The Right Bank or the Wrong Bank?

There are many Christians, churches, ministers, and leaders still pitching their tents and camping on the wrong bank of the river. We have a lot of believers still in Gilgal, Bethel, Jericho, and Jordan, talking about the arrival of the double-portion anointing and never being a part of it. These individuals realize the change that is coming upon the church and the land, but because of their protocol, habits, traditions, and rigid styles of worship, they are unable to be a part of the movement of God.

> And it came to pass, when the LORD would take up Elijah into heaven by a whirlwind, that Elijah went with Elisha from Gilgal.

And Elijah said unto Elisha, Tarry here, I pray thee; for the LORD hath sent me to Bethel. And Elisha said *unto him, As* the LORD liveth, and *as* thy soul liveth, I will not leave thee. So they went down to Bethel.

And the sons of the prophets that *were* at Bethel came forth to Elisha, and said unto him, Knowest thou that the LORD will take away thy master from thy head to day? And he said, Yea, I know *it*; hold ye your peace.

And Elijah said unto him, Elisha, tarry here, I pray thee; for the LORD hath sent me to Jericho. And he said, *As* the LORD liveth, and *as* thy soul liveth, I will not leave thee. So they came to Jericho.

And the sons of the prophets that *were* at Jericho came to Elisha, and said unto him, Knowest thou that the LORD will take away thy master from thy head to day? And he answered, Yea, I know *it*; hold ye your peace.

And Elijah said unto him, Tarry, I pray thee, here; for the LORD hath sent me to Jordan. And he said, *As* the LORD liveth, and *as* thy soul liveth, I will not leave thee. And they two went on.

And fifty men of the sons of the prophets went, and stood to view afar off: and they two stood by Jordan.

2 Kings 2:1-7

The sons of the prophets were in the same predicament. They knew and realized in Bethel, in Jericho, and in Jordan, that Elijah, a type of the single-portion anointing, was about to depart and that there was to be a new arrival of a double-portion anointing. But instead of being a part of the double-portion anointing, they were on the wrong bank of the river publicizing and heralding the arrival of the double-portion anointing. There will be men and women in this end time who will publicize and herald the prophetic, yet never be a part of it. Why? Because they are on the wrong bank. When you are on the wrong bank, all you do is complain, murmur, grumble, backbite, and get jealous of others on the right bank. When you begin to find yourself operating in these works of the flesh, ask yourself this question: "On which bank of the river am I?"

This question is out for the church. Which bank of the river are you on? Are you on the wrong bank or the right bank? Are you on the bank of the single-portion anointing or on the bank of the double-portion anointing? God is calling men and women to leave their bank of tradition and return to the place of the double-portion.

> **And it came to pass, as they still went on, and talked, that, behold, there appeared a chariot of fire, and horses of fire, and parted them both asunder; and Elijah went up by a whirlwind into heaven.**
>
> **And Elisha saw it, and he cried, My father, my father, the chariot of Israel, and the horsemen thereof. And he saw him no more: and he took hold of his own clothes, and rent them in two pieces.**
>
> **He took up also the mantle of Elijah that fell from him, and went back, and stood by the bank of Jordan;**
>
> **And he took the mantle of Elijah that fell from him, and smote the waters, and said, Where is the LORD God of Elijah? and when he also had**

**smitten the waters, they parted hither and
thither: and Elisha went over.**

2 Kings 2:11-14

This is what happens when you are on the right bank of the
river. You are never a viewer of the double-portion anointing,
but you are a participant and a partaker of the anointing.

**And when the sons of the prophets which *were*
to view at Jericho saw him, they said, The spirit
of Elijah doth rest on Elisha. And they came to
meet him, and bowed themselves to the ground
before him.**

2 Kings 2:15

Do you notice what is happening here? When you partake
of the double-portion anointing, it will be obvious and visible
to other believers — men and women will respect, bow to and
honor you when the anointing is visible in your life. Why?
Because the gift of God in you is making room for you. So
church, get your tent and camp off of the wrong bank of the
river and pitch it on the right bank of the river.

How to Change

In order for the church to fully flow with the change of the
Holy Spirit, *each believer must learn to open the garden of
his or her heart to biblical change.* We must repent and turn
away from every tradition, mechanism, style, and operation
that is not in line with God's Word.

**I am come into my garden, my sister, *my*
spouse: I have gathered my myrrh with my
spice; I have eaten my honeycomb with my
honey; I have drunk my wine with my milk: eat,**

O friends; drink, yea, drink abundantly, O beloved.

Song of Solomon 5:1

Second, *the Body of Christ must learn to impose ruthlessness on its attitude, behavior, character, style of life and things that are not according to God's Word.* It must be our heart cry to let go of anything in us that is not of God.

Third, *the nature of change is reciprocal.* If you have to talk change, then you must be ready to change.

Fourth, *the Body of Christ must develop a strong desire to listen.* For a change to be effective, Christians must learn to listen to one another. Shut up and listen. Many believers desire to change, but they never listen to their leaders and those in authority. As a result, required strategies and instructions of change have been neglected and abandoned. Many Christians hear noises and never listen. We must ask the Spirit of God to open our ears so that we can hear clearly what God is saying to the church today.

Fifth, *take correction and run with it.*

A reproof enters deeper into a man of understanding than a hundred lashes into a [self-confident] fool.

Proverbs 17:10 AMP

A single rebuke does more for a person of understanding than a hundred lashes on the back of a fool.

Proverbs 17:10 NLT

Like an earring of gold or an ornament of fine gold is a wise man's rebuke to a listening ear

Proverbs 25:12 NIV

Better is open rebuke than hidden love.

Proverbs 27:5 NIV

**The rod and reproof give wisdom,
But a child who gets his own way brings shame to his mother.**

Proverbs 29:15 NASB

**It is better to listen to the rebuke of a wise man
Than for one to listen to the song of fools.**

Ecclesiastes 7:5 NASB

CHAPTER FOUR

WAYS TO DEVELOP SPIRITUAL ACCURACY

There are some things that we must do to develop a lifestyle of moving or flowing in the spirit of accuracy. Accuracy in the things of God does not just happen overnight. It takes work and time. It takes a lot of personal commitment. The first thing to do in order to develop spiritual accuracy is to be divinely connected, hooked up to and mentored by seasoned, accurate men. Note the words "connected," "mentored," and "seasoned." These are very important words. We must learn to be connected. We must plug our spiritual cables into the right sockets of men who are seasoned, accurate and matured. We must be immersed into the connection. While this is important, it is paramount to understand that the process of every connection involves the ascertaining of how seasoned an individual is. It would be extremely detrimental to be connected or hooked up with a man who is out of season. It will eventually destroy the call of God upon your life.

There are many ministers and leaders within the church who are out of season. They are not operating in the right season. They are outdated. They do not know nor understand the various time zones of God. It is just like a man dressing in his summer clothes for the winter, or in his winter clothes for the summer. There is a great contradiction. The correct individual to be connected to must understand and discern the times and seasons of God. Their heart must be flexible and succulent in order to flow and change with the seasons of God.

If you wanted to learn a skill or a trade, you would definitely not want to be trained by an amateur or one who is not knowledgeable in that skill or trade. You would prefer to be trained by someone who possesses that particular skill. It would be foolish for an individual who wants to learn the trade of a mechanic to go to a baker. Also, it would be wrong for an individual who wants to learn how to repair BMW automobiles to go to a school where Honda repairs are taught.

It is important that the Body of Christ understands this. There are many Christians who are called into various positions and offices by God but who are being mentored and connected to the wrong ministries and churches. If God called you to be a prophet, the best way to start is to allow yourself to be mentored by seasoned prophetic men who have walked in the prophetic anointing. Also, if God calls you to be a pastor, evangelist, teacher, or an apostle, it would be more profitable to be connected with someone who does exactly what God called you to do.

We have many Christians in the wrong ministries. We have many believers who are connected, hooked up with and mentored by the wrong ministry and leader. We must discover the purpose of God for our lives, and get connected with men and women with similar purposes. We have prophets today being mentored by evangelists. We have evangelists being mentored by teachers. In order to achieve the optimum point of your calling and ministry, you must learn to be properly connected or hooked up with the correct ministry, and the right leader, who is doing exactly what God has called you to do.

You can be called to become a prophet, evangelist, pastor, apostle, or teacher. However, if your mentor is not seasoned and accurate, you will find yourself operating inaccurately in the things that you have been called to. It is vital that you ascertain whether your mentor is seasoned or not. Check out what spiritual time zone he or she is operating in. It is easy to discover this if you are not blind to the tradition and protocol of the church, ministry, and leader. All you need to do is listen to the words that come out of his or her mouth. Watch the ministers who are invited to preach in his or her church. Listen to some of their past and present tapes, and read some of their books. These steps will help you detect immediately what time zone your mentor is operating in. The time zone an individual operates in will determine his or her accuracy. One cannot be accurate if he or she is still operating from an outdated time zone.

We have believers, today, who desire to hear and understand the voice and direction of God, but who are being taught and trained by men and women who are deaf and dumb with regard to what God is saying. These believers are continually hooked up, connected, and mentored by people that are blatantly inaccurate in the ways of God.

Every believer today must learn to find someone that he or she knows is doing what God has told them to do; not just knowing what God told them to do, but *doing* it correctly. We must study these individuals from front to back, and back to front. We must study their ways, their acts, their exploits, their defeats, their walk and their victories. We must understand what makes them tick. We must study their ministries; we must understand what they are doing. If each believer would genuinely yield to the direction of the Spirit of God, God would lead them to seasoned, sharp and accurate men and women whose lives pattern the call of God upon them.

Let's look at the life of Elijah and Elisha:

> **And the LORD said unto him, Go, return on thy way to the wilderness of Damascus: and when thou comest, anoint Hazael *to be* king over Syria:**
>
> **and Elisha the son of Shaphat of Abelmeholah shalt thou anoint *to be* prophet in thy room.**
>
> **So he departed thence, and found Elisha the son of Shaphat, who *was* plowing *with* twelve yoke *of oxen* before him, and he with the twelfth: and Elijah passed by him, and cast his mantle upon him.**

> **1 Kings 19:15, 16b, 19**

Notice carefully what happens here. Elisha had to be anointed to be prophet in Elijah's room before a divine connection and mentoring could take place. In other words, Elisha had to be called into the office of a prophet. Once the calling is identified, the connection and mentoring becomes much easier. There are many ministers who want an office or position, and yet, they are not called to that office. Just because someone else is a prophet, they think they have to be one. God is tired of copycats. It is deadly and dangerous to walk in another man's office. Before you get connected and hooked up to a particular ministry, make sure you share in the mantle over that ministry.

> So he departed thence, and found Elisha the son
> of Shaphat, who *was* plowing *with* twelve yoke
> *of oxen* before him, and he with the twelfth: and
> Elijah passed by him, and cast his mantle upon
> him.

1 Kings 19:19

As Elijah passed by Elisha, the Bible says that Elijah cast his mantle upon Elisha, indicating that he, Elisha, was to follow him. Elisha made preparation to leave at once. Notice the spiritual connection here. Elisha immediately got connected and hooked up with the prophetic anointing on the life of Elijah. Elijah, who himself was a seasoned accurate man, mentored and turned Elisha into a spitting image of what an accurate man looks like.

Elisha followed Elijah. He learned his ways, ministry, thoughts, operation, and administration. In the long run, after the departure of Elijah, Elisha was able to walk in the footsteps of Elijah.

> He that receiveth a prophet in the name of a
> prophet shall receive a prophet's reward; and
> he that receiveth a righteous man in the name of
> a righteous man shall receive a righteous man's
> reward.

Matthew 10:41

The church must be properly taught concerning how to receive the ministry gifts. The Bible lets us know that he who receives a prophet (or any of the ministry gifts) would also receive the reward upon that prophet or that ministry gift.

There are ministry gifts with good and bad rewards. The church must be able to recognize these individuals. If you receive a ministry gift, or get connected with an individual that has good rewards upon his life and ministry, that reward will rub off on you. But if you receive and get connected with a ministry gift or an individual with a bad reward, that negative reward will also rub off on you. This is why the church needs to be very careful from whom they receive.

You can receive the spirit of an individual by reading his or her books, by watching that person on television, listening to their tapes, or by sending financial support to that person's ministry. Whatever rewards that person has whether bad or good, will rub off on you. This is why we need to be hooked up and get ourselves connected with sharp, accurate men—so that we can be able to receive from their lives and ministries.

When you find the correct ministry or the individual to be connected with, your spirit will leap inside of you with joy. You will then know that you need to study that ministry, or the life of that individual. What you do is, you begin to buy that person's tapes and books. You don't just study anybody's ministry or life for study's sake. You must be led.

One of the reasons the church has attempted many things and failed is because we have not been accurate in what God is saying. The church has more uncompleted projects than completed projects. We hear leaders say, "God said this must be done at this time." He or she begins with great eagerness and, after a couple of weeks, the project or idea is abandoned. We hide under the auspices of saying, "God is no longer leading in that direction." You must be sure about what you are doing before launching out into a project. Be very sure that God is leading you.

You can easily detect the symptoms of accuracy when an individual begins to learn to obey his own word. A lot of people are not in line with their own words. They cannot keep a promise. Their words return to them void. They do not accomplish what they say they will do.

Finding Your Way of Operation

The second thing that every believer must do is to find his or her own method of operation. Every believer must learn to discover the operation of the Spirit for their lives. Many believers will learn to become more accurate in the spirit realm once they know their own operations. If the Body of Christ would learn its operation and administration in the Spirit, the Body of Christ would be more accurate and sharp in pinpointing what God is saying and doing. If you study the life of Oral Roberts, Benny Hinn, Kenneth Hagin, and T. L. Osborn, you would find that each of these ministers of God have their own different operations and administration in the Spirit. One is forceful in the Spirit, while the other is kind of meek and gentle in his operation. Yet, they all fulfill the same function and accomplish the same goal.

If you try to enter an operation that is not yours, you will not be able to operate. The Body of Christ needs to ascertain what it takes to get the individual believer in the spirit. For some Christians to be in the spirit, they have to do a lot of worshiping. Others believe in fasting first, before any meeting. Find out what your operation is. You cannot afford to copy someone else's operation in this movement of the Spirit of God.

The reason that most of us are not accurate and cannot pinpoint in the spirit is because we have not learned to discern how the Spirit operates through us. We have had accidents with it, but we have not made a science out of it. Every now and then, something will happen without us getting into the flow of it. God wants to teach the church His administration and operation so that the church can be able to move into the spirit realm. Your accuracy will only come as a result of the filling up of the Word.

Time of Intimacy

Third, every believer must learn to spend quality time in the Word. Time must be given to the studying of God's Word. It is in spending time in God's Word that we learn how God speaks, how He moves and operates. We get acquainted with His ways through spending time in His presence. Intimacy with the Father in prayer and in the Word sharpens our accuracy level in the spirit.

> **Study to shew thyself approved unto God, a workman that needeth not to be ashamed, rightly dividing the word of truth.**
>
> **2 Timothy 2:15**

A lazy Christian cannot be accurate in the spirit realm. It takes mental discipline and diligence to be accurate in the spirit. The reason most believers cannot be accurate is because they cannot get the last thought out of their minds long enough to allow the new thought to enter into their minds. Most Christians are mentally lazy. We are not disciplined. We are not willing to study. Most Christians are not willing to control their wandering minds and gain focus.

The problem is not that God is not speaking, but that the Body of Christ is refusing to gain focus and eradicate the other thoughts from their minds.

The Right Atmosphere

Another way to develop spiritual accuracy is that we must learn how to properly create the right atmosphere. Atmospheric spirits can hamper a believer from hearing and understanding what God is saying and from discerning the expectations of God.

> **While he yet spake, there came from the ruler of the synagogue's *house certain* which said, Thy daughter is dead: why troublest thou the Master any further?**
>
> **As soon as Jesus heard the word that was spoken, he saith unto the ruler of the synagogue, Be not afraid, only believe.**
>
> **And he suffered no man to follow him, save Peter, and James, and John the brother of James.**
>
> **And he cometh to the house of the ruler of the synagogue, and seeth the tumult, and them that wept and wailed greatly.**
>
> **And when he was come in, he saith unto them, Why make ye this ado, and weep? the damsel is not dead, but sleepeth.**
>
> **And they laughed him to scorn. But when he had put them all out, he taketh the father and the mother of the damsel, and them that were with him, and entereth in where the damsel was lying.**

And he took the damsel by the hand, and said unto her, Talitha cumi; which is, being interpreted, Damsel, I say unto thee, arise.

And straightway the damsel arose, and walked; for she was *of the age* of twelve years. And they were astonished with a great astonishment.

Mark 5:35-42

When Jesus was about to raise Jairus' daughter from the dead, the first thing He did was to put everybody out of the room except Peter, James and John—because the atmosphere was not correct. The atmosphere was filled with doubt. Some Christians are not bold enough to get their atmosphere right. God cannot speak in a faulty atmosphere. Most Christians expect to hear from God when their atmosphere is polluted with strife, jealousy, envy, animosity, doubt, and other works of the flesh. We have to learn how to create the proper atmosphere in order to operate accurately and be able to hear what God is saying. We must create an atmosphere that is free from any satanic disturbances, and cause it to be conducive to an accurate Word of the Lord.

Sometimes, the reason we are not hearing accurately is because we are hanging around the wrong people. When God was ready to speak to Moses, He took him to the mountaintop. Sometimes God will have to take you out of certain atmospheres to speak to you. A wrong atmosphere will affect your ability to receive. And when you cannot receive, you cannot impart people.

Fresh Commitment to Spirit Use

Another way of developing spiritual accuracy is to understand that a fresh consecration, dedication, and commitment releases fresh oil.

> But my horn shalt thou exalt like *the horn of* an unicorn: I shall be anointed with fresh oil.

Psalms 92:10

Being filled with the Holy Spirit is not something that happens to us just one day. It is something that needs to happen to us all of the time. As believers, we need our oil changed constantly. We need a freshness in our walk and relationship with God. Ongoing freshness and newness in our walk opens our hearts to discern and hear more clearly from the Lord.

Flowing From Your Inner Man

> For as many as are led by the Spirit of God, they are the sons of God.

Romans 8:14

Finally, every believer must learn to work and flow out of his or her recreated human spirit, and not out of his or her head. The days of flowing from our heads are over. The church must now flow accurately from its spirit. A man or woman that flows from his or her head is bound to be inaccurate in the ways of the Spirit. The "Deep" has to call the deep things of God. Accuracy is birthed as a result of flowing in the realm of the Spirit. Accuracy is never birthed by walking in the flesh.

To request a complete catalog featuring books, videotapes, compact discs, and audio tapes by Dr. John A. Tetsola, or to contact him for speaking engagements please write or call:

ECCLESIA WORD MINISTRIES INTERNATIONAL
P.O. BOX 743
BRONX, NEW YORK 10462

Phone: (718) 904-8530
Fax: (718) 904-8107

Please visit our website at www.ecclesiaword.org or you may send an email to reformers@msn.com.